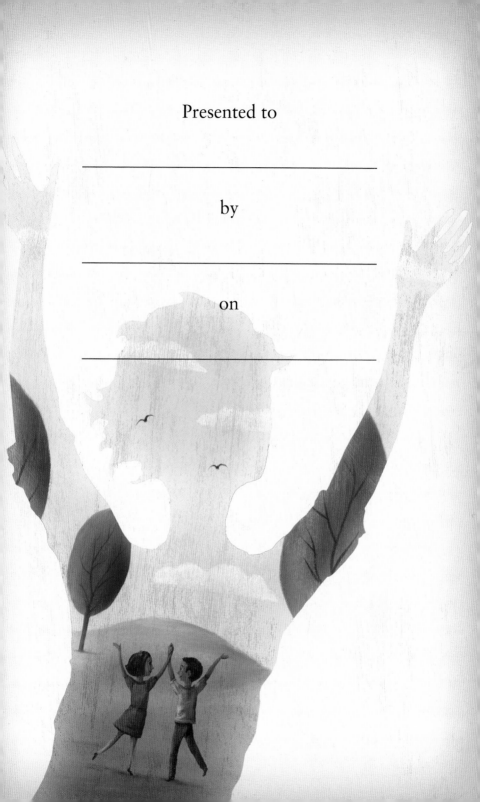

Presented to

_____

by

_____

on

_____

ZONDERKIDZ

A Believe Devotional for Kids: Think, Act, Be Like Jesus
Text copyright © 2015 by Randy Frazee
Illustrations copyright © 2015 by Steve Adams

ISBN 978-0-310-75202-8

Requests for information should be addressed to:
Zonderkidz, 3900 Sparks Drive SE, Grand Rapids, Michigan 49546

Art direction/design: Cindy Davis

Printed in China

15 16 17 18 19 20 21 /LPC/ 9 8 7 6 5 4 3 2 1

A BELIEVE DEVOTIONAL FOR KIDS

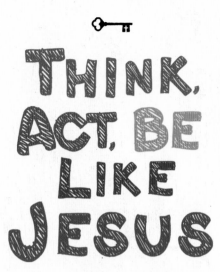

THINK, ACT, BE LIKE JESUS

90 Devotions

written by RANDY FRAZEE

illustrated by STEVE ADAMS

ZONDERkidz

Table of Contents

THINK

ACT

THINK

LIKE

JESUS

GOD

The heavens tell about the glory of God.
The Skies show that his hands created them ... Their
voice goes out into the whole earth. Their words go out
from one end of the world to the other.

—Psalm 19:1, 4

Galaxies upon galaxies stretch out in space.

The water cycle sustains all the plants and animals
on earth.

The systems of veins and arteries in our bodies keep
us alive.

God shows his work in big and small ways. Think about
how large the oceans are but how much detail your
fingerprints have. Picture the Rocky Mountains and then
the delicate parts of a snowflake.

God shows himself clearly in these amazing creations.
There is no reason to doubt him. The apostle Paul wrote,
"Ever since the world was created it has been possible
to see the qualities of God that are not seen. I'm talking
about his eternal power and about the fact that he is God.
Those things can be seen in what he has made."
(Romans 1:20)

Dear God,
help me to see your presence in
the world around me, in the people
I know, and in myself.

GOD

*Choose for yourselves right now who you
will serve ... as for me and
my family, we will serve the LORD.*

—*Joshua 24:15*

Moses had given the Israelites the Ten Commandments.
Still, some of them broke their promise to God and
started worshiping idols. It seems strange that anyone
could bow down in front of a gold cow or statue, but we
have to choose who we will serve, just as the people of
Israel did. Do we serve other people or things? Or do we
serve the one true God?

Joshua was the leader of the Israelites after Moses.
Joshua was in charge of leading the people into the
Promised Land. God was with them during that time.
He fought for them as they began to take over the land.
With Joshua to lead them, the Israelites stayed devoted to
God. Near the end of his life, Joshua knew he would die
soon. He gathered the people together. He told them they
would need to choose for themselves to serve the Lord, the
one true God.

We have the same challenge. We need to make decisions
when we get out of bed, are at school, serve at church,
play with our friends, and even decide what to eat. Are we
serving God, ourselves, or something else?

Dear God,
I promise to serve you,
and only you.
You are the one true God.

GOD

*The fire of the L*ORD *came down. It burned up the sacrifice. It burned up the wood and the stones and the soil. It even dried up the water in the ditch.*

—*I Kings 18:38*

⟨⟩

Yes, you read that right! God's fire "dried up the water."

Elijah and the worshipers of Baal had a kind of contest. They each wanted to prove their own god was the most powerful. The showdown had been strong. From morning until noon, the followers of Baal had asked their god to burn up their offering. They shouted for Baal and danced for him, but nothing happened. Baal didn't do anything.

The one true God didn't need to be asked a second time. Elijah set up a sacrifice on an altar and soaked it with water. God's fire burned Elijah's sacrifice. And then it burned part of the stone altar. And the altar had been wet! Elijah really wanted to prove a point—and he did.

Let's thank God for the times when he has clearly shown himself in our lives. And let's look for him to do so again today.

Dear Lord,
thank you for being a part
of my life. Please continue
to show me who you are and
who you want me to be.

GOD

So I gave you a land you had never farmed.
I gave you cities you had not built. You are now
living in them. And you are eating the fruit
of vineyards and olive trees you did not plant.

—*Joshua 24:13*

Do you make sure to tell people thank you? Are you surprised when people do or don't say thank you to you?

One reason we don't always thank others is that human beings tend to feel entitled. That means we feel like we should get all sorts of things even if we didn't earn them or don't really deserve them.

Another reason might be that we take things for granted. In some places, people can't be sure they will have food, clean water, or be safe. But most of us are sure of getting those things, so we don't worry about them. We are certain we will have them.

We also forget what life was like before we walked with Jesus. We forget that everything we have is a gift from God.

The most important thing that God gives us is knowledge of Him. We don't deserve to know God, but he still lets us. May we always remember that knowing the gospel is pure grace—a gift from God.

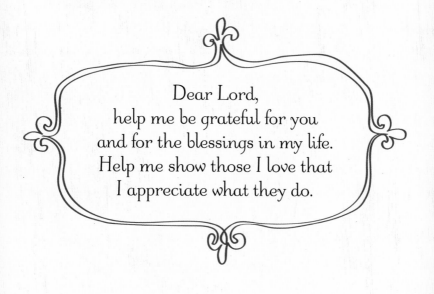

Dear Lord,
help me be grateful for you
and for the blessings in my life.
Help me show those I love that
I appreciate what they do.

GOD

Joshua made a covenant for the people ... he reminded them of its rules and law ... Then he got a large stone. He set it up in Schechem under the oak tree. It was near the place that had been set apart for the LORD.

—*Joshua 24:25–26*

When God has just done something amazing for us, we act grateful. We decide to be better people, do nice things, and obey all the rules. We might think that we will change forever and never go back to doing bad things. But after a little while, we may simply forget God's goodness or what we decided to do.

Joshua understood that people are like that. "He got a large stone ... [and] set it up" in a place where the people would see it. The stone was to help his people remember their promises to God. Joshua said, "This stone will be a witness against us ... the stone will be a witness against you" (Joshua 24:27).

Nothing in our lives is more important than our relationship with God. What will you use to remind yourself of God's faithfulness? And how will you keep your faithfulness to him?

Dear God,
thank you for loving me and
caring about me. Thank you for
being faithful to me. I promise
to do my best to always be
faithful to you.

PERSONAL GOD

I think about the heavens. I think about what your
fingers have created. I think about the moon and
stars that you have set in place. What are human beings
that you think about them? What is a son of
man that you take care of him?

—Psalm 8:3–4

Has there been a time when you felt God with you? Have you felt his power and love? Have you felt his hope and strength? Feeling God with you might make you want to sing and shout for joy.

David wrote songs all throughout his life. He wrote psalms when he was a shepherd looking at the billions of stars God created. He wrote songs when he was a fighting warrior and when he was king of Israel. The songs of David are very personal. They show his personal relationship with God. You can have that kind of relationship with God too.

Like a shepherd, the Lord wants to protect us. He wants to give us things, show us the right ways, and help us when we need it. Then we can say, like David, "The LORD is my shepherd. He gives me everything I need" (Psalm 23:1). Our good Shepherd longs to have his "goodness and love … follow [us] all the days of [our] life" (v. 6). What a blessing!

Dear Lord,
thank you for being a personal
God who cares about me, protects
me, and loves me. Thank you
for always being with me.

19

PERSONAL GOD

Since God is on our side, who can be against us? ...
Who can separate us from Christ's love? Can trouble or hard
times or harm or hunger? Can nakedness or danger or war?

—Romans 8:31, 35

God is always on our side. He gave his only Son to die for us. To pay for our sins. What amazing love!

Some people try to run away from this love, or they don't believe in it. But can we be separated from the love of Christ? In Romans 8, the apostle Paul tells us absolutely not!

God's written Word also shows us how much he loves us. It says: "Not even death or life can separate us from God's love. Not even angels or demons, the present or the future, or any powers can separate us. Not even the highest places or the lowest, or anything else in all creation can separate us. Nothing at all can ever separate us from God's love." (Romans 8:38–39). What amazing love!

Dear God,
your love is amazing! Thank
you for loving me so much that
nothing can ever separate us.

PERSONAL GOD

"I know the plans I have for you," announces the LORD.
*"I want you to enjoy success. I do not plan to harm you. I will
give you hope for the years to come."*

—*Jeremiah 29:11*

The kingdom of Judah had turned away from God.
Jeremiah was a prophet. He warned the people that
the Lord was going to punish them for turning away
from him. The punishment? The Babylonians attacked
Jerusalem three times and carried off some of the people.
Jeremiah wrote the letter above to the people who had
been carried off to remind them that God still had a good
plan for their lives.

Did that letter make the people feel good or bad? Did they feel hopeful? And what about us? Whatever our situation, do we feel hope that God has good things coming for us?

God's written words to his people should make us hopeful that he will keep his promise.

Dear Lord,
I know you have good things planned for me, even though bad things may come my way too. Thank you for keeping your promises and giving me hope.

SALVATION

The LORD *God said, "Just like one of us, the man can now tell the difference between good and evil."*

—Genesis 3:22

Adam and Eve sinned in the Garden of Eden. They were tricked by the serpent and ate the fruit that God had forbidden them. So they were thrown out of the garden and they were made to feel pain and hardship for the rest of their lives. And the relationship between God and his people was broken.

But God had a plan to fix his relationship with his people. He sent his Son to take the punishment for the sins of the world. Jesus died for our sins so that our relationship with God could be healed. And then something amazing happened. Jesus rose from the dead.

The angels at Jesus' empty tomb said: "Why do you look for the living among the dead? Jesus is not here! He has risen! Remember how he told you he would rise. It was while he was still with you in Galilee. He said, 'The Son of Man must be handed over to sinful people. He must be nailed to a cross. On the third day he will rise from the dead!'" (Luke 24:5–7).

How amazing! Humans broke their trust with God, but he loved us so much that he sent his Son to save us anyway.

Dear God,
sometimes I do the wrong thing,
but you keep on caring about
me. Thank you for your grace!

25

SALVATION

"The fire and wood are here," Isaac said. "But where is the lamb for the burnt offering?" Abraham answered, "God himself will provide the lamb for the burnt offering, my son."

—Genesis 22:7–8

Abraham and Sarah waited twenty-five years to have a baby. Twenty-five years! That's nothing to God, but it's a long time for parents who really want a child.

They waited, and God came through. But then he asked Abraham to do a really scary thing. He asked Abraham to kill his own son. He asked Abraham to offer his son as a burnt offering instead of the usual lamb. In the end, God saved Abraham's son because Abraham proved he had faith in the Lord.

Later, God's people had waited hundreds of years for the Messiah. He was going to be a great leader who would free them from their enemies. They waited for hundreds of years. And then they only had Jesus with them for three years!

God's people waited, and God came through. But then he did a really scary thing. He let people kill his own Son. God gave up Jesus as an offering for our sin. He did what he couldn't make Abraham do, and he did it because he loves us so much.

Really, God? *Yes, really. Because I love you.*

Dear God,
thank you for loving us so much
that you would give up your only son.
Thank you for wanting us to be free
of sin and to live with you in heaven.

SALVATION

The LORD will go through the land to strike down the Egyptians. He'll see the blood on the top and sides of the doorframe. He will pass over that house. He won't let the destroying angel enter your homes to strike you down.

—Exodus 12:23

Abraham's descendants—the people in his family born after him—went to Egypt. They moved there because there was not enough food in their homeland. God's people lived in Egypt for four hundred years. The king of Egypt, called Pharaoh, made them his slaves. Then God delivered Moses. He told Moses to take his people out of slavery and lead them to the Promised Land.

But Pharaoh would not let the people leave. To show Pharaoh his power, God sent ten plagues. These were bad things that happened just to the Egyptians, not to the Hebrews.

Before the final plague, God told his people that he would kill the firstborn son in every house in Egypt. To protect themselves, the Hebrews needed to put the blood of a lamb on their doorframes. God would pass over those houses. The blood would save the people within from death.

Hundreds of years later, the blood of Jesus Christ also saved people. Jesus bled so that we could be saved from our sins.

Lord,
I know you can do anything you want. You saved Moses and his people from Pharaoh. And you saved the rest of us from our sins. Thank you for using your power to help us.

29

SALVATION

The servant was pierced because we had sinned. He was crushed because we had done what was evil ... The LORD has placed on his servant the sins of all of us.

—Isaiah 53:5–6

It's not fair.

Jesus hadn't broken any laws. And if Jesus was the Son of God, and he wasn't able to sin, Jesus was falsely accused. Then he was punished by people who were breaking the law.

It's not fair!

He had healed and fed, freed and forgiven. But "people looked down on him. They didn't accept him" (Isaiah 53:3). No angels came to help as Jesus was "led away like a lamb to be killed" (v. 7). And the sins he died for were ours!

It's not fair!

But it was God's good plan. We have broken plenty of his laws. We are guilty of lots of things. We should have died on the cross. But Jesus did instead. Not us. Jesus was sacrificed. Not us.

It's not fair … It's grace—a gift.

Dear Jesus,
you gave up everything to save me. You didn't deserve to die on the cross, but you did it because you love me. Thank you for your incredible gift.

THE BIBLE

*God's power has given us everything we need
to lead a godly life. All of this has come to us
because we know the God who chose us.*

—2 Peter 1:3

Just by looking at the natural world all around us, we
can know there is a God. (Roses and wombats don't just
show up on their own!) But how can we learn about God?
How can we learn his plans for us? How do we know how
he wants us to behave? We learn these things by reading
God's written Word, the Bible.

The apostle Peter wrote that God has given us "everything
we need to lead a godly life." God helps us know him
through his Word. If you read the Bible, you can know
that we are all sinners. We all make big and small mistakes. But because Jesus died for us, it's okay. God forgives
our sins.

So the Bible shows us about ourselves and about our God.
If you read the Bible, "may more and more grace and
peace be given to you. May ... you learn more about God
and about Jesus our Lord" (2 Peter 1:2).

Dear God,
guide me as I read the Bible to
learn more about you and your
plan for me. Show me the things
I need to know to live in a
way that pleases you.

THE BIBLE

I am the God of your father. I am the God of Abraham. I am the God of Isaac. And I am the God of Jacob.

—Exodus 3:6

The Bible has many stories of God speaking to people. Sometimes he spoke with words you can hear. Other times, people heard them only in their minds or while they were dreaming.

While Moses was taking care of some sheep, he noticed a burning bush. The bush looked like it was on fire, but it didn't burn up. Then Moses heard God speak his name. Once God got Moses's attention, he told him who he was.

And he said, "I have seen how my people are suffering in Egypt. I have heard them cry out because of their slave drivers. I am concerned about their suffering" (Exodus 3:7). Our kind God acted because he loved his chosen people.

Then God told Moses about his important job. "I am sending you to Pharaoh. I want you to bring the Israelites out of Egypt. They are my people" (v. 10). God would help Moses become a strong leader because he loved Moses.

In the same way, God's plan for us is based on his love for us. And as his Word explains, his plan for us—for our good—is to love him with all we are, to love our neighbor as ourselves, and to be people of prayer and worship, joy and hope.

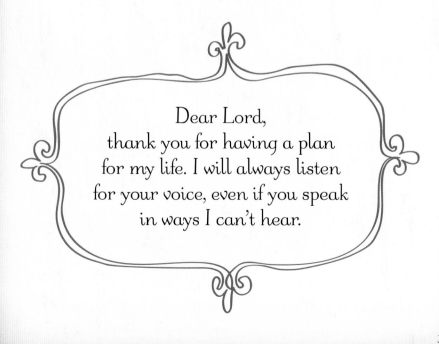

Dear Lord,
thank you for having a plan
for my life. I will always listen
for your voice, even if you speak
in ways I can't hear.

THE BIBLE

We told you about the time our Lord Jesus Christ came with power.
But we didn't make up clever stories when we told you about it.
With our own eyes we saw him in all his majesty.

—2 Peter 1:16

What do you believe? People can tell you anything. But that doesn't mean it's true. Lots of people write things on websites, in newspapers, or talk on TV, but how do you know if you can trust their words? You have to know how to tell what is true from what is made up.

We can believe what we read in God's Word for quite a few reasons. First, God has made sure the writings of the Bible have been well-kept for thousands of years.

Second, people who actually saw things happen wrote the gospel books. Finally, many people who put God's Word onto paper willingly died rather than say that Christ didn't rise from the dead. People don't die for made-up stories or fairy tales.

Still, untrue teachings were brought into the early church. Some followers started not to follow God's Word. In the verse, Peter wrote to believers to bring them back to the truth about Jesus.

We can trust the truth of Scripture. So why don't we?

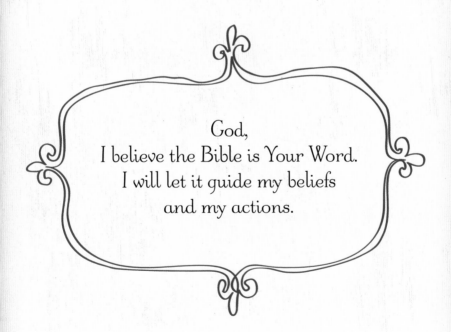

God,
I believe the Bible is Your Word.
I will let it guide my beliefs
and my actions.

IDENTITY IN CHRIST

This is my convenant with you. You will be the father of many nations. You will not be called Abram anymore. Your name will be Abraham, because I have made you a father of many nations.

—Genesis 17:14–5

During Bible times, a person's name was more than just a way to find someone. The name described something about that person. In the Old Testament, we read that Esau means "hairy." Esau's hairiness played an important part in his life story (see Genesis 27:11–23). In the New Testament, we read that Barnabas means "son of help" (Acts 4:36). And Barnabas was a helper.

When we read that God gave a person a new name, he was changing their mission or place in life. God changing *Abram* (meaning "Exalted father") to Abraham (meaning "father of many"). The meaning of the name *Abraham* points to God's plan to make *Abraham's* children into the great nation of Israel.

Now think about this. If you have received Jesus as your Savior, your new names are *Forgiven, Redeemed, Chosen, child of God, light of the world, salt of the earth,* and *Beloved.* God has changed your mission and place in life. What are you doing to live up to your new names?

Dear Lord,
help me find my mission and my
place through my faith in
Jesus Christ. Help me become
a true child of God.

IDENTITY IN CHRIST

Some people did accept him and did believe in his name. He gave them the right to become children of God.

—John 1:12–13

⟨∾⟩

We are children of God. And that means God is our heavenly Father. What that means to you may depend a lot on your earthly father.

Maybe you were blessed with a father who shows you how much he loves you; a father whom you can turn to in tough times.

Not everyone on this planet has that kind of earthly father, however. Sometimes dads aren't there for you and don't show their love. Some people may have dads who do the opposite.

Your experiences with your earthly father might make it hard to trust your heavenly Father. But know that in the Lord you can experience great healing, grow in trust, and one day run to him for help and protection. God will help you.

Dear God
you are my heavenly Father.
I will trust in you and love you
because I know you love me.

IDENTITY IN CHRIST

But God chose you to be his people. You are royal priests.
You are a holy nation. You are God's special treasure. You are
all these things so that you can give him praise. God brought you
out of darkness into his wonderful light.

—1 Peter 2:9

We all have times when we were chosen ... or not
chosen. Not chosen until last to be on the kickball team.
Not chosen as a partner for a class project. Not chosen
for the church play.

These moments can change us. Perhaps we don't try so
hard anymore. What's the point? On the other hand, if
we are picked for something, we may feel like we can do
anything.

Being chosen by God can also change us. Peter called us
"his people ... a holy nation ... God's special treasure."
What amazing grace to be chosen! What a privilege to be
"holy," to be set apart to serve our God! And what an
honor to be special to the King of kings!

The beautiful thing is that all those who welcome Jesus
as their Lord can accept a new self through him. We are
chosen! We can praise God as we live each day secure in
his love.

Dear Jesus,
thank you for choosing me!
Thank you for making me special
and loved in your eyes.

CHURCH

"But what about you?" [Jesus] asked. "Who do you say I am?" Simon Peter answered, "You are the Messiah. You are the Son of the living God."

—Matthew 16:15–16

The question that Jesus asked Peter is a question every one of us needs to answer. Who do we say Jesus is? What do we say or do to show the world who our savior is?

Peter answered that question. He shared directly with Jesus his belief that Jesus was actually "the Messiah, the Son of the living God." When Jesus heard that bold statement, he proclaimed, "On this rock I will build my church" (v. 18). More than two thousand years later, people still say that Jesus is the Son of the living God. We continue to tell our faith in Jesus.

We are to proclaim that Jesus is God's Son, who gave his life so we would be forgiven.

Who will you share that message with today? Also, take time to thank someone who shared the gospel message with you.

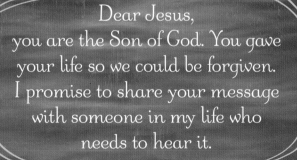

Dear Jesus,
you are the Son of God. You gave
your life so we could be forgiven.
I promise to share your message
with someone in my life who
needs to hear it.

CHURCH

*On that day the church in Jerusalem began to be
attacked and treated badly. All except the apostles were
scattered throughout Judea and Samaria.*

—*Acts 8:1, 4*

After Jesus was raised from the dead, the rulers of the
Jewish church were mad about the message stated by
followers of Jesus. Stephen was one of those faithful
followers. He told how the Jewish people had mistreated
the prophets God had sent them. The reaction of the
people was to stone him to death. Stephen's death marked
the beginning of "a great persecution." Believers in
Jerusalem needed to run away because they were in
danger. They ran to places throughout southern and
central Israel.

But because they had to run away, the gospel was spread
to those other places. Jesus' order to the first disciples was
to spread the Good News. He wanted them to build his
church beyond Jerusalem. And that was what was
happening.

What in your life looks a little scary right now? Know
that God can use it for your good, just as he used the
harassment of his people in Jerusalem so long ago.

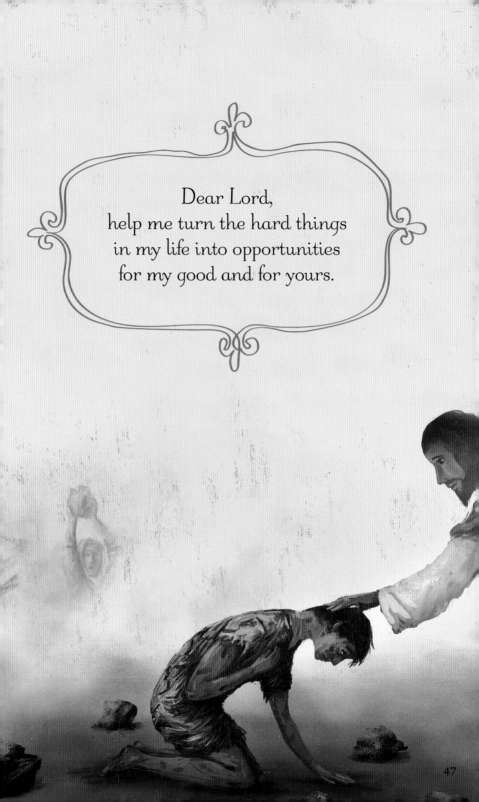

Dear Lord,
help me turn the hard things
in my life into opportunities
for my good and for yours.

CHURCH

Listen, fellow children of Abraham! Listen, you Gentiles who worship God! This message of salvation has been sent to us. My friends, here is what I want you to know. I announce to you that your sins can be forgiven because of what Jesus has done. Through him everyone who believes is set free from every sin. Moses' law could not make you right in God's eyes.

—Acts 13:26, 38–39

Among the people you know, who is on your "Least Likely to Accept Jesus" list? In the early church, Saul may have been at the top of many people's lists. He stood by calmly, coldly, as Stephen was stoned to death. He was obsessive in his hunt of Jesus' followers and his mission "to destroy the church" (Acts 8:3).

But on the road from Jerusalem to Damascus, Saul met the risen Jesus. In that moment, Saul gave his life to Christ. From then on he devoted the rest of his days to building Christ's church. Paul was a great preacher. He took the gospel to the non-Jews. And he explained to his fellow Jews how Jesus fulfilled Old Testament prophecies about a Messiah.

Among the people you know, who do you think will never name Jesus as Savior and Lord? You may be wrong just as people were wrong about Saul. Don't give up!

Dear God,
please show me how I may be able
to share your Word with the
person in my life who needs it most.

HUMANITY

Certain people have secretly slipped in among you …
They are ungodly people. They misuse the grace of our God …
They say no to Jesus Christ, our only Lord and King … How
terrible it will be for them! They have followed the way of Cain.

—Jude 4, 11

Jude was both a half-brother and a follower of Jesus. In the verses above, he warned Christians in the early church about false teachers. These false teachers were trying to convince believers that being saved by grace meant they could sin however they wanted. Jude noted that these dangerous teachers had "followed the way of Cain." This means the way of selfishness and greed (shown by Cain's careless, thoughtless offering to the Lord in Genesis 4). And the way of hatred and murder (shown by Cain's killing of his brother Abel, also in Genesis 4).

The need to know the Scripture is essential. Knowing the Bible helps us recognize false teachers (see Acts 17:11) and our own sins. So ask God to show you in what ways you are taking "the way of Cain." Also ask the Lord to continue to work in your heart. Ask him to make you more selfless and generous, more loving and gracious, more like Jesus.

Dear Lord,
guide me in doing what is right and
following the perfect example set
by your Son, Jesus Christ.

HUMANITY

When Israel was a young nation, I loved them.
I chose to bring my son out of Egypt. But the more I called
out to Israel, the more they went away from me.

—Hosea 11:1–2

In this passage, God speaks of his relationship with Israel as a naughty son. God wanted his people to understand what they were doing. They were straying away from him.

In Hosea 11, God thought back over all he had done for his chosen people. He often helped them even when they didn't know he was with them. Out of love, he rescued them from slavery in Egypt. Israel was about to go into captivity again, this time enslaved by the mighty nation of Assyria. Because Israel walked away from the Lord by worshipping idols, lying, and rebelling, he would punish them.

Hear the Lord's heartbreak: "I taught Ephraim to walk. I took them up in my arms … I led them with kindness and love" (vv. 3–4). As their devoted Father, God sees that "My people have made up their minds to turn away from me" (v. 7).

Yet God stated once again his love. "My heart is stirred inside me. It is filled with pity for you. I will not be so angry with you anymore" (vv. 8–9). God loves us with the same kind of unending, undeserved love.

Dear God,
thank you for always loving us,
even when we don't respect you
and love you the way we should.

COMPASSION

When they cried out to you again, you heard them from heaven. You loved them very much. So you saved them time after time.

—Nehemiah 9:28

Throughout their history, the Israelites struggled to stay true to God. Sometimes they followed God. But then they would sin and rebel again. The pattern could not be avoided. Israel followed God. Israel turned from God. God sent enemies to attack. God rescued Israel. Israel followed God. Israel turned from God. Over and over again, it was repeated.

No matter how often Israel "did what you did not want them to do," prompting the Lord to "[hand] them over to their enemies," he responded with love whenever they cried out to him (v. 28). The God who calls us to show love is not asking us to do anything he himself hasn't done. Our God showed love to Israel again and again. Our God shows love to us again and again and again.

God's love is constant. Since the days of ancient Israel up through today, God offers his people relief from the misery caused by their own sin.

Dear Lord,
your grace and mercy are
incredible gifts to us, gifts we don't
always deserve. Thank you for
your everlasting love.

COMPASSION

Everyone has sinned. No one measures up to
God's glory. The free gift of God's grace makes us right
with him. Christ Jesus paid the price to set us free.

—Romans 3:23–24

Compassion means "suffer with." God calls us to be with
people who are suffering and suffer with them so they are
not alone. It doesn't mean we can fix the problem. It does
mean we can feel a bit of their pain.

God has always graciously shown compassion for his
people. The final compassion was sacrificing his Son,
Jesus Christ. Humankind had sinned. People had sinned
so much that the only right punishment was death. But
because of his compassion, God offered Jesus as a substitute
for us. Jesus took the place for sinful humanity. Through
this one act, God showed his complete compassion.

We can reflect God's nature when we show compassion to
others. Who in your world today needs a touch of compassion from you?

Dear God,
please help me show compassion
to someone in my life today, someone
who really needs a friend or a
shoulder to cry on.

COMPASSION

*When you are gathering crops in your field, you might
leave some grain behind by mistake. Don't go back to get it.
Leave it behind for outsiders and widows. Leave it for children
whose fathers have died. Then the Lord your God
will bless you in everything you do.*

—*Deuteronomy 24:19*

God is gracious and compassionate. So we shouldn't be
surprised that God made laws for his people that call us
to be like him. Israelites were called on to be kind to
foreigners and friends alike. God set up specific plans for
helping the poor and those in need, just like the one in the
verse above.

Deuteronomy 24:19 is a simple instruction. But it suggests
much about acts of compassion. If I choose to think of
others and don't pick up every sheaf of grain, will I have
enough grain for myself? Clearly, compassion can cost.
Compassion can mean making sacrifices. And
compassion may mean taking a step of faith.

The compassion of Christ-followers today is just as
important. As Jesus himself said, "Everyone will know
that you are my disciples, if you love one another"
(John 13:35).

So who will you show love to today?

Dear God,
guide me as I try to become a
more compassionate person,
someone who always thinks
of others before myself.

COMPASSION

My dear brothers and sisters, pay attention to what I say.
Everyone should be quick to listen. But they should be slow
to speak. They should be slow to get angry.

—James 1:19

Compassion was not written about in the Old Testament.
Not at all! But Jesus told stories that taught the importance
of compassion. And letters written to the young church
by the apostles added real instructions. Look at some of
James's specific how-tos in the verse above for living this
new life in Christ.

Being "quick to listen" and "slow to speak" means really
listening to people in order to hear their heart. Careful
listening will help us to react with compassion that makes
an important difference in people's lives.

Here's how we can put compassion into practice:

"Here are the beliefs and way of life that God our Father
accepts as pure and without fault. When widows are in
trouble, take care of them. Do the same for children who
have no parents" (v. 27).

"'Love your neighbor as you love yourself.' ... If you really
keep this law, you are doing what is right" (2:8).

Dear Jesus,
help me to be more like you—
compassionate, thoughtful,
and a good listener.

COMPASSION

*Which of the three do you think was a neighbor
to the man who was attacked by robbers?*

—Luke 10:36

❧

A Jewish man had been robbed, beaten, and left for dead
on the lonely road. A priest saw the man and passed on the
other side. He didn't want to be late!

An expert in the law of the church also noticed the bleeding
man and passed by on the other side. He needed to get to
the temple!

Then a Samaritan man—an enemy of the Jewish people—
walked by, felt sorry for the injured man, drove him to a
local hotel, and left money to care for him.

Who did the right thing? Who was the injured man's
neighbor? The expert in the law to whom Jesus was telling
the story of the Good Samaritan answered correctly. The
neighbor was "the one who felt sorry for him." And Jesus
then spoke words to that expert that apply to us as well:
"Go and do as he did" (v. 37). Don't make excuses. Don't
explain why you "can't" help. And don't let serving God
keep you from serving your neighbor.

Dear God,
I promise to serve my neighbor,
whether that person lives next
door or down the street or nowhere
near me. I will show love and
give help to people in need.

STEWARDSHIP

It's possible that you became queen for a time just like this.

—Esther 4:14

❧

The word *stewardship* probably sounds pretty funny. Mostly this means that we are responsible for caring for something. It might mean that we should take care of the earth. Or that we need to care for other people around us. Stewardship also relates to opportunities God gives us.

The beautiful young Esther became wife of King Xerxes and queen of Persia. But no one knew she was also Jewish. At that time, the Jews had been taken out of Israel. They lived in Persia with people who were not children of God. When a law to "destroy, kill and wipe out all the Jews" was made (Esther 3:13), God's plan for Esther became known. Her uncle Mordecai asked Esther if it was possible that God had led her to become queen to help save her people. Esther had a job to do, and she bravely did not turn away from it.

Think about the opportunities to serve God in your life. Are there opportunities in your family or neighborhood, church or school, sport or other activities? Ask God to show you what opportunities he is giving to you. Can you make a difference in a person's life and bring glory to God? Then, as you step into those situations, you can know that the Lord is with you.

Dear God,
please show me how I can serve you
in my everyday life. I want to bring
you glory no matter what I'm doing.

STEWARDSHIP

I prayed for this child. The L*ORD* *has given me what
I asked him for. So now I'm giving him to the* L*ORD*.
As long as he lives he'll be given to the L*ORD*.

—*1 Samuel 1:27–28*

Every child ever born was created by our heavenly Father.
So every child ever born is the Lord's. He trusts children to
their parents' care, but the children always belong to the
Lord.

An Old Testament mother named Hannah completely
understood this idea. For the longest time, Hannah could
not have children. She pleaded with the Lord for a child.
When God granted Hannah's wish, she named her son
Samuel. Once Samuel was old enough to leave his mother,
Hannah "[gave] him to the L*ORD*." Hannah let Samuel
grow up in the temple so that he could serve the Lord.
Hannah realized that Samuel had always belonged to the
Lord anyway.

Hannah's story shows us that we all belong to the Lord. We
are his possessions, placed here on earth to help do his will.

Dear Lord,
I believe everything I am and
everything I own belongs to you.

STEWARDSHIP

No one can serve two masters at the same time. Either you will hate one of them and love the other. Or you will be faithful to one and dislike the other. You can't serve God and money at the same time.

—Luke 16:13

How do you use your money? Jesus warned us that money can take over God's place in our life. One of Jesus' disciples added that "love for money causes all kinds of evil." (1 Timothy 6:10).

To loosen our hold on money, God challenges us to honor him with our money. If we fail to return to the Lord a part of what he has provided for us, we rob him. Everything we have is ultimately from him.

Money has a lot of power. It can be used for good or for evil. The ultimate goal is to use God's resources, not to help ourselves, but to help others and to serve God.

For your good and God's glory, loosen your hold on money. It will loosen its hold on you.

Dear Lord,
help me use my money wisely
to help others and serve you.

ETERNITY

Christ died for our sins ... He was buried. He was raised from the dead on the third day ... He appeared to Peter. Then he appeared to the 12 apostles.

—*1 Corinthians 15:3–5*

❧

The tomb was empty? What had happened to Jesus' body?

Some people say that Jesus was not raised from the dead. They say that the chief priests paid the soldiers who had been guarding the tomb to say that the disciples had stolen the body. If that had happened, the soldiers should have lost their lives for failing at their assignment!

Also, Paul tells us that the resurrected Jesus appeared to Peter, to the disciples, "to more than 500 brothers and sisters at the same time" (v. 6), and to Paul himself. Why did no one among those 513 people deny Paul's report of seeing Jesus?

And if the resurrection was a lie, why would so many Christians die rather than deny that Jesus had risen from the dead?

Be encouraged in your faith. Do not be afraid to share the gospel. Our resurrected Lord has opened the door to eternity.

Dear Jesus,
I believe you lived, died, and
rose again all to save me from sin.

ETERNITY

Death, where is the victory you thought you had?
Death, where is your sting?

—1 Corinthians 15:55

Why are people afraid to die? Many non-Christians say it is because they fear what comes after death or that they don't think anything comes after death.

Why don't Christians fear death? Many Christians say it is because they know what good things await them after death because of their belief in Christ.

And what a life that will be! The author who wrote *The Lion, the Witch, and the Wardrobe*, C. S. Lewis, wrote this in one of his books: "All loneliness, angers, hatreds, envies, and itchings that [our earthly life] contains, if rolled into one single experience and put into the scale against the least moment of the joy that is felt by the least in Heaven, would have no weight that could be registered at all."

We should not fear death. We can instead joyfully look forward to eternal life with Jesus.

Dear Jesus,
I believe that after I die
I will come to live with you in
heaven forever. Thank you for
saving a place for me.

ACT
LIKE
JESUS

WORSHIP

*The jailer called out for some lights. He rushed in,
shaking with fear. He fell down in front of Paul
and Silas. Then he brought them out.
He asked, "Sirs, what must I do to be saved?"*

*They replied, "Believe in the Lord Jesus.
Then you and everyone living in your house will be saved."*

—Acts 16:29–31

What a weird question for a jailer to ask two prisoners! But
these weren't just any two prisoners. The jailer had noticed
something different about them.

Paul and Silas had been arrested, beaten, and thrown into
prison. But, they were still praying and "singing hymns to
God" (Acts 16:25). Then an earthquake shook the prison.
The chains on all the prisoners fell off, but none of them
ran away. Talk about weird!

We often need to worship in the dark as Paul and Silas
did. "The dark" might be times when we worship even
though we are worried, scared, or confused. Other people
will notice that we trust in God through good times and
bad. People will notice that we bless the name of the Lord
whether he gives to us or takes away. They may even join
together with us in worship!

Dear God,
I promise to praise you even when times are hard. I know that you will take care of me.

WORSHIP

*Think about things that are in heaven. That is where
Christ is. He is sitting at God's right hand. Think
about things that are in heaven. Don't think about
things that are only on earth.*

—Colossians 3:1–2

There's a challenge for you: think about doing all the things
that you need to today with your heart and mind focused
on "things that are in heaven." Imagine doing everything as
an act of worship and service that pleases our Lord!

Going to school, doing your homework, finishing your
chores—you can do all these things as acts of worship.

The things that we do in our home and at school, we can
do with a thankful heart. In our church and out in the
community, we can do everything with gratefulness. And
we can ask for the Lord to lead us and to give us strength
and joy. Whatever we are doing, our love for our heavenly
Father should keep us constantly talking with God. And
that is worship!

Dear Lord,
help me worship you with
everything I do.

WORSHIP

Aaron's sister Miriam was a prophet.
She took a tambourine in her hand. All the women
followed her. They played tambourines and danced.

—Exodus 15:20

When we worship God, we can show our love for our Creator, our heavenly Father.

So why don't we—like Miriam—give everything we can during our worship time? Why do we hold back? Are we embarrassed to sing out loud? Does it seem scary to get up and worship the Lord with our whole body? Are we worried what other kids will think about us? Whatever the reasons, God can help us relax and worship him without worry.

Maybe you really want to grab a tambourine when you think about God's work in your life. Maybe you wish you could celebrate God just like Miriam and hold nothing back. Maybe the secret is … just do it!

Dear God,
thank you for everything you do
for me. I want to worship you like
Miriam did with my heart,
body, and soul. Please help me
do so, even if it's when no one
else is watching.

WORSHIP

Daniel found out that the king had signed the order.
In spite of that, he did just as he had always done before ...
He got down on his knees and gave thanks to his God.

—*Daniel 6:10*

The king of Persia made a law that for thirty days people could only pray to him. Daniel knew this law could not be changed. Daniel knew that disobeying the law would mean being thrown into a den of hungry lions.

And yet, three times a day, Daniel prayed to his God just as he "had always done before." Despite the law, Daniel was committed to worshipping God.

Can you do the same thing? Will you announce your faith right now by going to church, reading the Bible, or talking to friends about Jesus? Will you continue to follow him no matter what might happen?

Dear Lord,
I know that you are the one true
God. I will keep my faith in
you no matter what comes my way.

PRAYER

It was very early in the morning and still dark.
Jesus got up and left the house. He went to a place
where he could be alone. There he prayed.

—Mark 1:35

When you think of people who pray a lot, who do you think of? Do you think of Mom or Dad, Grandma or Grandpa? Do you think of a character you've read about or seen? Do you think of people in the Bible?

The Bible shows many examples of people who prayed a lot. But there is a no more perfect example than Jesus. Spending time with his Father in prayer gave him strength. It helped him understand what he needed to do here on earth. If Jesus needed to turn to his Father for strength and help, how much more do we need to!

"Get up half an hour earlier and spend some time with the Lord!" "Before you watch TV, spend some time in prayer." The suggestions go on and on. Sometimes we struggle when it comes to sticking to a plan and giving up other things we like. But our heavenly Father will gladly help us stick to our prayer time with him. Ask him!

Dear God,
help me find the time to pray every
day. I want to grow closer
to you and seek your guidance.

PRAYER

Lᴏʀᴅ, how long must I wait?
Will you forget me forever? How long will you
turn your face away from me?

—*Psalm 13:1*

Have you ever prayed like that? Have you ever asked God if he doesn't care for you or why he's left you alone? Yes, it's allowed. All of us can and should pray like that. When you pray, you should feel like you can be honest and open with God. In fact, that kind of prayer is not only allowed, but it is important to having a real relationship with God.

Our God isn't a far-off "being" somewhere out there in outer space. He is a good Father who longs to be with his children even when they're hurt or angry. God isn't worried by our questions and doubts. We don't have to put on a fake happy face to please him. He lets us be honest about our worries, our fears, and what we're disappointed about.

So, just like David in Psalm 13, tell God what is in your heart. Like David, you can be sure that God wants to know what is going on in your life. He longs to hear you speak to him from your heart.

Dear Lord,
thank you for listening to
my prayers, even when I'm worried
or upset. I know you'll answer
me in the right way.

PRAYER

Don't be too quick to speak. Don't be in a hurry to say anything to God. God is in heaven. You are on earth. So use only a few words when you speak.

—Ecclesiastes 5:2

Yes, our heavenly Father wants to hear from us. He wants us to be open and honest with him. He cares about our hurts and disappointments. Even our disappointments in him. We can spill our hearts to him. But, we also need to listen to Solomon's point in the verse about prayer.

Solomon wrote that when we pray we should make listening to God an important part of the prayer. Just like sheep follow a shepherd's voice, we need to listen to God, who is leading us. Remember, Solomon was supposed to be the wisest man who ever lived. So we should learn from his words.

God wants to hear from us (2 Chronicles 7:19; Psalm 88:2; Luke 18:1). He also wants us to hear from him (2 Timothy 3:16–17).

God gives us the privilege of speaking to him. When we speak to God, it shouldn't just be something that we do because a parent or pastor tell us to. It should be something we do because we want to be near to God—to listen to him and to tell him the truth about ourselves.

Dear God,
just as you always listen to
me when I pray, I will always
listen to you.

PRAYER

Don't worry about anything. No matter what happens, tell God about everything. Ask and pray and give thanks to him.

—Philippians 4:6

This is many people's favorite verse for a good reason. Philippians 4:6 is about real life, and saying "don't worry" admits that there is much in life that can cause worry.

The verse is practical. It gives us a plan for when we are tempted to feel anxious. The plan? Pray for anything and everything, and always pray with thanks. We may not be able to be thankful *for* the situation, but that is not the command. We can always be thankful *in spite* of the situation. We can be thankful to be a child of our good, gracious, perfect heavenly Father.

Philippians 4:6–7 makes a promise. "Then God's peace will watch over your hearts and your minds. He will do this because you belong to Christ Jesus." The peace of God comes when we stop worrying and think of our all-loving, all-wise God.

Dear God,
thank you for taking away my
worries and fears. I know that by
praying to you with thanks I can
overcome the obstacles in my path.

BIBLE STUDY

[Ezra] read the Law to them from sunrise until noon ...
He read it to the men, the women, and the children old
enough to understand. And all the people paid careful attention
as Ezra was reading the Book of the Law.

—Nehemiah 8:3

"From sunrise till noon." What was your first thought when you read those words? Maybe "That's way too long!" or "There's no way I can read that long!"

Do you sometimes get bored when you sit through a sermon in church? Do you wish the pastor would get on with it already? Do you ever feel the same way in school?

What a sharp difference from Ezra's attention "from sunrise until noon"! That is five or six hours! Clearly, these people were hungry for God's Word. They spent six hours hearing a priest read Scripture. But more happened than reading and listening. The people were living and doing what the Scripture told them to do. One time, Nehemiah reported, the people "listened while the Levites read parts of the Book of the Law of the LORD their God. They listened for a fourth of the day. They spent another fourth of the day admitting their sins. They also worshiped the LORD their God." (Nehemiah 9:3).

This week, whenever you open the Bible, pretend you're hearing the words for the first time. And pray to the Holy Spirit to help you truly hear them. And then live them!

Dear Lord,
I promise to read the Bible today
and hear your Word. Then I will
put that Word into action.

BIBLE STUDY

Your word is like a lamp that shows me the way.
It is like a light that guides me.

—Psalm 119:105

"Oh! I didn't see that!" It's easy to bump into things in the dark. Everyone can make mistakes if they don't have the right tools, like a flashlight. The same is true in life.

Thankfully, God has supplied us with his Word to light our path. Just like a lamp, God's word can show us the way we are supposed to go. But it only works if we carry it with us all the time. We don't need to literally carry a Bible in our back pocket. (Though that's not a bad idea.) But we need to carry God's word in our hearts. We need to believe his lessons and continue to follow him. Otherwise we might go down the wrong path or trip and fall.

We can end up setting down God's light because of sin, lies, and upside-down values. But we must always keep the light of God's Word with us if we are to make it to our next step in life.

Dear God,
you are the light in my life.
Guide me down the path I am
meant to walk and keep me
from the darkness.

BIBLE STUDY

*Teach me to live as you command
because that makes me very happy.*

—*Psalm 119:35*

❧

There are 66 books in the Bible. There are 1,189 chapters, 31,173 verses, and 773,692 words.

The Bible is the actual Word of God. God gave us his words for a reason. The ancient stories and words on these pages can help us go down the right path to where God wants to take us.

Even more important is what happens in our hearts as we walk with the Lord. The Holy Spirit uses God's Word to teach us. He also uses its truth in our hearts to change us. He wants to make us more like Jesus himself—compassionate, kind, patient, loving, and obedient.

So study those 66 books, 1,189 chapters, 31,173 verses, and 773,692 words, and you will be changed.

Dear God,
thank you for giving us the Bible.
Guide me as I read your Word
so I can become more like Jesus.

BIBLE STUDY

Israel, listen to me. The Lord *is our God. The* Lord *is the one and only God. Love the* Lord *your God with all your heart and with all your soul. Love him with all your strength. The commandments I give you today must be in your hearts. Make sure your children learn them.*

—*Deuteronomy 6:4–7*

A recent newspaper headline said: "Americans Love the Bible but Don't Read It Much." Why don't people read their Bibles anymore?

For many years, the words of God and the stories of his people were passed down by word of mouth. People told Bible stories to each other. Then Moses wrote down the first five books of the Bible. Even after Moses wrote these down, not everyone had their own copy. People still had to tell each other the truth of God's Word.

What an amazing privilege and duty—to share with others the good news of God's love for them! Make sure you keep it up.

Dear Lord,
I promise to read your Word
and share it with the people I know.

BIBLE STUDY

Make sure you obey the whole law my servant Moses gave you. Do not turn away from it to the right or the left. Then you will have success everywhere you go. Never stop reading this Book of the Law. Day and night you must think about what it says. Make sure you do everything written in it.

—Joshua 1:7–8

We don't always find it easy to do what our teachers say, to obey our parents' rules, or even listen to our friends' advice. We all feel like we know best. We don't want anyone telling us what to do. And yet God's Word includes many chapters telling us to learn the Lord's law and live them out.

After Moses died, God visited Joshua. Joshua was the new leader of God's people. God reminded Joshua why it was important to read God's Word and to follow it. As James, the brother of Jesus put it, "Don't just listen to the word … You must do what it says" (James 1:22). God's people are to learn his Word and live it.

Dear God,
help me live my life according
to your law. I want to live in
a way that honors you.

BIBLE STUDY

A farmer went out to plant his seed … But the seed that fell on good soil is like those who hear the message and understand it. They produce a crop 100, 60 or 30 times more than the farmer planted.

—*Matthew 13:3, 23*

What does a plant need to grow? Air, water, soil, and sun.

What do followers of Jesus need to grow? First, we need to watch out for evil that would take the truth from us. Second, we need to understand the Bible so we don't get confused about what is true. Third, we also need to stay far away from doing things that keep us from living the way God wants.

With the story in the verse above, Jesus reminds us that we need to have the right attitude when we hear or read God's Word. If we are open to hear God's words, they will make a real difference in our lives and change us for the better.

Dear Jesus,
show me how to be like you—
how to believe truly, understand
God's Word, and live the
way I should.

SINGLE-MINDEDNESS

I am the Lord *your God. I brought you out of Egypt. That is the land where you were slaves. Do not put any other gods in place of me.*

—*Exodus 20:2–3*

What do you spend a lot of your time at home doing? Are you playing a computer game? Are you on your tablet? Are you on the Internet looking at things you want to buy?

It can be hard during the school week to focus on what really matters. You have school during the day. And then maybe you have sports or music or dance after school. Perhaps you're in Girl or Boy Scouts. Maybe you have a family dinner to go to and then homework to do after that. And then you just want to relax, right? Don't you deserve a little computer time? Or a little time texting with friends? But God wants us to be more single-minded than that.

To be single-minded means to have one goal above all others. One focus. From the beginning God made it clear that his people's main focus should be him.

Dear God,
help me focus on what is
important in life—talking
with and learning from you.

SINGLE-MINDEDNESS

Israel, listen to me. The LORD is our God. The LORD is the one and only God. Love the LORD your God with all your heart and with all your soul. Love him with all your strength.

—*Deuteronomy 6:4–5*

In the Ten Commandments, God tells us to serve only him. He told the Israelites he had earned their trust in this way because he rescued them from Egypt.

An expert in the law "tested" Jesus by asking what he thought was the greatest of the Ten Commandments. "Jesus replied, 'Love the Lord your God with all your heart and with all your soul. Love him with all your mind'" (Matthew 22:37). These old words, said again by Jesus, are still the most important for us thousands of years later.

So how do we love the Lord with all that we are? We should expect to see God at work in our life. Even if we are busy or scared or frustrated, we should try to see God everywhere we are and in everything we are doing. Let's ask the Holy Spirit to train us to see signs of God in our everyday life. When the Holy Spirit shows us God's presence with us, how could we respond with anything other than grateful love?

Dear Lord,
I promise to try to love you
just as Jesus did, with all my
heart, with all my soul,
and with all my mind.

SINGLE-MINDEDNESS

Don't worry about your life and what you will eat or drink.
And don't worry about your body and what you will wear.
Isn't there more to life than eating? Aren't there more
important things for the body than clothes?

—Matthew 6:25, 27

Food and clothing are pretty important parts of life. Maybe you've never had to worry about having enough food to eat or clothes to wear. But many people around the world are uncertain every day if they will have them.

You may have worried about things like your grades in school. Or you might have stressed out over not having the next best video game. Or you've worried you won't be good enough in soccer.

If God tells us not to worry about necessary things like food and clothing, do you really think you should be worried about all that other stuff?

We can find reasons to worry about all sorts of things, but everything on your worry list can be taken care of by this truth that Jesus taught: your heavenly Father knows what you need (see Matthew 6:32).

Choose to trust that God your Father is able to provide all you need.

Dear God,
you know what I need in life.
Help me see past the little things
and instead think about what
is truly important.

TOTAL SURRENDER

Some Jews ... Shadrach, Meshach and Abednego ... don't pay any attention to you, King Nebuchadnezzar. They don't serve your gods. And they refuse to worship the gold statue you have set up.

—Daniel 3:12

The people of Israel were not faithful to God. They disobeyed his commands. So, God removed his protection. As a result, Judah was invaded by the Babylonians. Many Hebrews had to leave their homes and were sent to Babylon.

Shadrach, Meshach, and Abednego were among those who were sent away. They were picked to be trained to serve the king. They were also forced to make an important choice: worship the one true God or follow the laws of Babylon to save their own lives.

Our idols are not always tall golden statues like the Babylonians worshiped. Our idols are more untouchable. They can be money, possessions, popularity ... But they raise the same issue for us that the statue did for Shadrach, Meshach, and Abednego: whom will we worship?

Shadrach, Meshach, and Abednego chose total surrender. By God's grace, may we do the same.

Dear God,
I dedicate myself to you.
You are the only
one I will worship.

TOTAL SURRENDER

Then Nebuchadnezzar said, "May the God of Shadrach, Meshach and Abednego be praised! ... They trusted in him. They refused to obey my command. They were willing to give up their lives. They would rather die than serve or worship any god except their own God.

—Daniel 3:28

Total surrender to God can completely confuse people who don't believe. In our world, we value being the biggest, the best, the first, and the one who has done whatever it took to get ahead!

Our actions as Christians that *attract* attention can also *direct* attention to God. Think about Shadrach, Meshach, and Abednego. They refused to bow and worship a statue of King Nebuchadnezzar.

Faithfulness to God can have a price. Nebuchadnezzar reminded Shadrach, Meshach, and Abednego that the cost of not worshiping his statue was being thrown into a blazing furnace. But the Jewish men simply said, "The God we serve is able to bring us out of it alive ... Even if we knew that our God wouldn't save us, we still wouldn't serve your gods. We wouldn't worship the gold statue you set up." (Daniel 3:18–18)

Later, Nebuchadnezzar praised God, the one true God the young men had trusted and who had delivered them.

Dear God,
help me to always be
faithful to you. And let
my faith help others see
your greatness.

TOTAL SURRENDER

I'll go to the king. I'll do it even though
it's against the law. And if I have to die, I'll die.

—Esther 4:16

❧

"He must become more important. I must become less important" (John 3:30). These are the words John the Baptist spoke about Jesus. Two thousand years later, those words offer a good life goal for every follower of Jesus. We become less of ourselves when we give our life for our God.

Queen Esther had kept her Jewish heritage a secret. But, she was ready to give her life for her people and for her God. Haman, the king's highest official, hated Mordecai (Esther's cousin). This was because Mordecai had refused to bow down and honor Haman. As revenge, Haman made plans to kill Mordecai and all the Jews in Xerxes' kingdom. Esther faced a difficult decision: protect her people or protect her position as queen and perhaps her own life …

Esther chose total surrender, and God protected her.

Are you ready to do the same?

Dear God,
show me how to be strong
and brave like Esther.
Show me how to surrender
to your will and your
plan for me.

TOTAL SURRENDER

While the members of the Sanhedrin were throwing stones at Stephen, he prayed. "Lord Jesus, receive my spirit," he said. Then he fell on his knees. He cried out, "Lord! Don't hold this sin against them!" When he had said this, he died.

—Acts 7:59–60

The last words a person speaks before they die can be heartbreaking, funny, wise, sad, or clever. In Stephen's case, they honored God.

Stephen was not an apostle, but he was a powerful witness for Jesus. "Stephen was full of God's grace and power. He did great wonders and signs among the people" (Acts 6:8). Conflict arose, arguments followed, and frustration grew wherever Stephen went. "But he was too wise for them.

That's because the Holy Spirit gave Stephen wisdom whenever he spoke" (Acts 6:10). One day, Stephen was unfairly taken before the Sanhedrin. He then put his total surrender to God on display.

Stephen told the story of the Hebrew people, from Abraham through Joseph. He told of Moses, the golden calf, the tabernacle, the prophets killed by Jewish leaders, and the murder of Jesus, Son of God, Messiah. What a gift Stephen left in his bold and God-honoring last speech!

Then, before he died, Stephen spoke as Jesus had from the cross: "Lord, don't hold this sin against them" (Acts 7:60).

May what we say and how we say it honor God. It shows both our obedience to him and our faith in him.

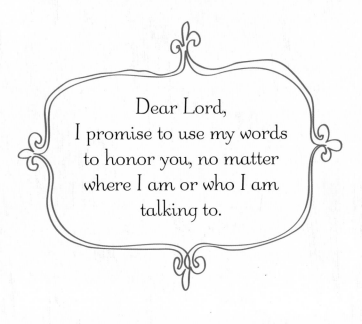

Dear Lord,
I promise to use my words to honor you, no matter where I am or who I am talking to.

BIBLICAL COMMUNITY

*The city wall was completed on the 25th day of the month
of Elul ... God had helped us finish the work.*

—Nehemiah 6:15–16

Have you heard the word *community*? If you have, maybe
you think of friends and neighbors. Our Biblical community
is those people who are also Christians who work together
to get something done for God. Your community may help
others or the church.

Nehemiah had to rely on his community too. He was living
far away from Jerusalem. Nehemiah learned that "the wall
of Jerusalem [was] broken down, and its gates have been
burned with fire" (Nehemiah 1:3). He was sad. He cried
and prayed. Then God acted. Nehemiah went back to
Jerusalem. He led others to rebuild the wall around the city.
The wall would protect his people from the bullying of the
other countries around them. Everyone in the community,
including children, was called to help with this big project.

This fifteen-foot thick wall was built in just fifty-two days
because the Biblical community worked together to make
it happen. What might God be asking you and your
community to do?

Dear Lord,
I want to be a part of your
community. Lead me to the
work you need done.

BIBLICAL COMMUNITY

There is one body and one Spirit. You were appointed to one hope when you were chosen. There is one Lord, one faith and one baptism. There is one God and Father of all. He is over everything. He is through everything. He is in everything.

—Ephesians 4:4–6

Imagine listening to a band playing a great piece of music. Now picture each member of the band playing their own instruments and making their own sounds. If we want the concert to be a success, each player's instrument has to be in tune. Each player must play with the other musicians, not just for himself.

We are the musicians. We should play a song of God's grace and joy to the world.

There are questions for us all. First, are we in tune with God? Do you listen to God? Are you doing God's will? And second, are we playing well with others? Does our playing give glory to God? Do you treat others as Jesus would?

God sent his Son to bring our lives back in tune with his. Jesus leads the song, teaching us to live well with each other. Let's play our parts in His song of joy. Let's get in tune with God and play together. Remember, other people are watching us.

Dear God,
let me live in harmony with the
people around me as we all
work to sing your praises.

BIBLICAL COMMUNITY

Don't be proud at all. Be completely gentle.
Be patient. Put up with one another in love.

—*Ephesians 4:2*

Our society is often entitled. Webster's dictionary defines this as "the feeling or belief that you deserve to be given something (such as special privileges)." This feeling implies self-love and self-centeredness. That's not a great way to think for a community, especially a Christian community.

Think about Paul's words in the verse above. Gentleness, patience, and a lack of pride are important traits that help us get along well with other people. To "put up with one another in love" isn't always easy, especially if those people are getting in the way of what we feel or believe we're entitled to!

But one of the big differences between the church and the rest of the world is Jesus' call to live for others. In the New Testament, followers of Jesus were urged to look out for one another. When the early Christians did this, people outside the church saw it and wanted to belong to the family of God. Looking out for one another could have the same effect on our community today.

So this week, start each day by asking God to show who he wants you to look out for, help, and serve.

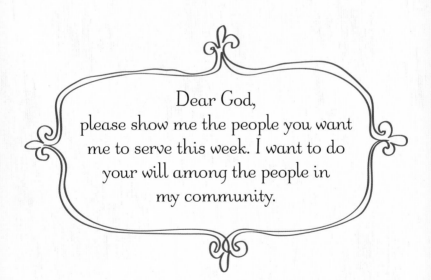

Dear God,
please show me the people you want
me to serve this week. I want to do
your will among the people in
my community.

BIBLICAL COMMUNITY

*The L*ORD *God said, "It is not good for the man
to be alone. I will make a helper who is just right for him."*

—Genesis 2:18

It must have been quite the parade in the Garden of Eden!
God brought every living creature to Adam to be named.
God had created an amazing number of birds, fish,
mammals, and other animals. But Adam had not found
himself a good helper. Not the bull. Not the ostrich. Not
the giraffe. Not even the golden retriever! Yet God knew
that "it is not good for the man to be alone."

God meant for humans to have relationships with each
other. And relationships would be made better by the
presence of God among them. God can make those
relationships happen for us today.

Dear God,
please help me strengthen my
relationships with my family and
friends. Help me treat them well
and never take them for granted.

SPIRITUAL GIFTS

[King Nebuchadnezzar] said to Daniel, "I'm sure your God is the greatest God of all. He is the Lord of kings. He explains mysteries. That's why you were able to explain the mystery of my dream."

—Daniel 2:47

In the days of King Nebuchadnezzar's reign over Babylon, God showed himself through miracles. God gave Daniel the power to understand complicated dreams. The king had people (astrologers) who told him what his dreams meant. He believed that dreams had meaning in real life. He threatened to kill these people "if [they] do not tell me what my dream was and interpret it" (Daniel 2:5).

That's a tall order! First, tell the king what he dreamed—and then tell him what it meant? As the astrologers said, "What the king asks is too difficult. No one can reveal it to the king except the gods" (v. 11).

Daniel learned from God both what the dream was and what it meant. Daniel went before the king, saying, "There is a God in heaven who reveals mysteries" (v. 28). Then Daniel explained the king's mysterious dreams.

More than once in the Bible, God shows himself as the one true God. He does this by blessing people with spiritual gifts. Praise God that he wants to be known and that he makes himself known!

Dear God,
thank you for making yourself
known to me and the other
Christians in the world. Please keep
demonstrating your love and
your glory to us.

SPIRITUAL GIFTS

But the Father will send the Friend in my name to help you. The Friend is the Holy Spirit. He will teach you all things. He will remind you of everything I have said to you.

—John 14:26

When Jesus ate the last supper with his disciples, he knew he would soon be put to death. He wanted his disciples to be encouraged and prepared for life without him. Jesus promised to send them the Holy Spirit. The Spirit would give them hope, guidance, and help to get through the hard days ahead.

Think about how this promise was fulfilled in the early church. The Spirit gave strength and courage to Peter (Acts 2), Stephen (Acts 7), and Paul (Acts 13). The Spirit helped them to be well spoken and convincing. The Spirit was a reminder of everything Jesus said.

Maybe you've had these kinds of moments with the Holy Spirit. Perhaps you knew the words you heard yourself say weren't your own. If you haven't felt the Holy Spirit, try doing something good and see what the Spirit does for you. Trust the Spirit to help us to be powerful witnesses for Jesus. We just have to take a step of faith and trust that the Spirit will speak through us.

Dear Lord,
let the Holy Spirit come to me
so I can experience the
promise Jesus made.

SPIRITUAL GIFTS

They saw something that looked like fire in the shape of tongues. The flames separated and came to rest on each of them. All of them were filled with the Holy Spirit. They began to speak in languages they had not known before. The Spirit gave them the ability to do this.

—Acts 2:3–4

Before he went up to heaven, Jesus told his disciples to wait in Jerusalem for the promised gift of the Holy Spirit. Ten days later, the Holy Spirit came on the Jewish celebration of Pentecost. The disciples were very brave, and the church was born.

Pentecost always falls fifty days after Passover. Pentecost honors when God gave the Ten Commandments to Moses at Mount Sinai.

Since that early time of the disciples, Pentecost has marked the beginning of the Christian church. Christians remember the giving of the Spirit, our comforter and helper who will never leave us.

As Jesus had told the disciples, "The harvest is plentiful, but the workers are few" (Matthew 9:37; Luke 10:2). But the Spirit-filled disciples were now in harvest mode. Join them by giving yourself up to the Spirit. He will let you know who needs to hear about Jesus. And he will help you to speak the truth with love.

Dear Holy Spirit,
I pray that you will show me
who in my life needs to hear the
good news of Jesus Christ, and
that you will help me tell them.

SPIRITUAL GIFTS

Peter said, "I don't have any silver or gold. But I'll give you what I do have. In the name of Jesus Christ of Nazareth, get up and walk." Then Peter took him by the right hand and helped him up. At once the man's feet and ankles became strong.

—Acts 3:6–7

Peter and John saw a crippled beggar outside the temple. He was unable to walk so others had carried him to the temple gate so he could beg.

Because Jesus had taught them compassion, Peter and John stopped when he asked them for money. They had no money, but they offered the man healing in the name of Jesus. And the man got up and was able to walk again.

We all have spiritual gifts we can use to help others. We may not have money, but spreading the Good News to others is a very important task. And if we don't share our spiritual gifts, what's the point of having them?

Trust yourself to God. Say, "Here I am! Send me!" No story is more wonderful that the one we as Christians can share. And nothing we can do is ever more important than sharing it.

Dear Lord,
help me to find my spiritual
gifts and use them to
bring about your plan.

OFFERING MY TIME

So the message from the Lord came to me.
The Lord said, "My temple is still destroyed. But you are
living in your houses that have beautiful wooden walls."

—Haggai 1:3–4

When the Jews came back from being held captive in
Babylon, one of their first jobs was to rebuild the temple and
restore worship to the one true God. They began strong—
but disagreement was also strong. The building project
completely stopped and no one worked on it for ten years!

Then the prophet Haggai delivered a message from God.
Haggai asked them why they were building their own
houses instead of the house of the Lord, the Almighty
One. God was the one who had brought them back to
Judah. What is wrong with this picture? Haggai wanted
to know. Why were they using their time so unwisely?

The truth that all time belongs to the Lord should definitely
control how we use that time. But that doesn't always
happen. What question about the use of your time would
Haggai ask you today? What activity is keeping you from
doing what God wants you to do?

Ask his Spirit to show you. Then ask him to provide the
wisdom you need to use time in a manner that pleases God.
"If any of you needs wisdom, you should ask God for it. He
will give it to you. God gives freely to everyone and doesn't
find fault" (James 1:5).

Dear Lord,
I offer my time to you. Please show me how to use my time in a way that pleases you.

OFFERING MY TIME

"Why were you looking for me?" [Jesus] asked.
"Didn't you know I had to be in my Father's house?"

—*Luke 2:49*

The things that we spend our time doing tell others what's important to us. What twelve-year-old Jesus did said a lot about what was important to him and what he thought was the best use of his time.

Jesus traveled to Jerusalem with family and friends for the celebration of Passover. The Passover celebration remembers how God rescued the Hebrews from slavery in Egypt. After the festival, young Jesus stayed behind in Jerusalem. After three days of searching, Mary and Joseph found their son—God's Son—"in the temple courtyard. He was sitting with the teachers. He was listening to them and asking them questions" (v. 46). Jesus asked his parents "Didn't you know I had to be in my Father's house?" (v. 49).

What time each day will you plan to be with Jesus, to study his Word and listen for his voice? That time will be more valuable to you and to the world than you can imagine. There is no better use of our time than spending it with our Savior, our Lord, our Shepherd.

Even at the young age of twelve, Jesus understood how best to use his time. The rest of us are still learning.

Dear Jesus,
I promise to take time
every day to talk with you,
listen to you, and study your Word.

OFFERING MY TIME

Keep in mind that I have given you the Sabbath day. That is why on the sixth day I give you bread for two days. Everyone must stay where they are on the seventh day. No one can go out.

—*Exodus 16:29*

The Sabbath is a gift from God. Like all his laws, his instructions for keeping the Sabbath are for our own good. In your church, the Sabbath may be Saturday or Sunday. But whatever day you observe the Sabbath, he who created us knows what is best for us. And he planned a day of rest, replenishment, refreshment, and renewal.

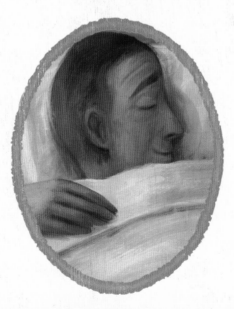

But sometimes we don't spend the Sabbath the way God wanted us to! Why? Maybe because we want to be lord of our life. We want to do what we want to do when we want to do it. We don't want someone telling us what not to do on a certain day. But keeping the Sabbath is key to living according to God's rhythm.

If taking a day of rest came easily, God would only have had to give nine commandments, not ten. Sometimes we might feel pressure to get things done, to go places, to stay busy, but observing the Sabbath is a step of faith. God will enable us to accomplish what we need to accomplish.

God created us with the need for regular and planned rest. Why aren't you doing it? And why not start?

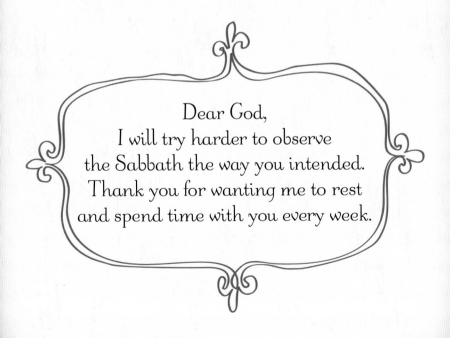

Dear God,
I will try harder to observe
the Sabbath the way you intended.
Thank you for wanting me to rest
and spend time with you every week.

OFFERING MY TIME

Jesus told them, "The time for me to show who I really am is not here yet. For you, any time would be the right time."

—John 7:6

Timing can be everything. That is true when you tell a joke. If you tell the funny part too soon, it might not make sense. Timing is important when you are baking something. And don't forget when you need to tell mom or dad that you didn't do so well on that test. It's by far better to do that when you catch them in a good mood!

Jesus wanted to be sure he was doing things at the right time. But Jesus also wanted to live according to God's timetable and no one else's. Not even his own.

This fact made Jesus rather mysterious. Sometimes it seemed to others that it was the right time to get attention for his cause. One time his brothers suggested that Jesus make his way to Judea in time for a major Jewish festival. The crowds would offer great advertising. In those pre-Twitter days, word of mouth was everything for a successful campaign.

Jesus told his brothers about an important idea in his life. He managed his priorities according to the timing of God the Father. Jesus kept God as his focus in everything he did, including how he managed his time.

Yet another lesson we can learn from Jesus.

Dear Jesus,
help me to manage my time,
whether that's doing homework,
spending time with friends and
family, or doing your work
and reading your Word.

GIVING MY RESOURCES

One person gives freely but gets even richer. Another person doesn't give what they should but gets even poorer.

—Proverbs 11:24

❧

One dollar out of every ten. *Okay, I can do that.*

Ten dollars out of every one hundred. *Umm. Okay ...*

A hundred dollars out of every thousand. *This is getting hard.*

A thousand out of every ten thousand? *That's a lot of money.*

In the Old Testament, God's people gave one-tenth of their crops, herds, and flocks for God's purposes. This is called tithing. Giving a tithe started as a nonreligious act. People in the ancient world gave a tribute tax of a tenth (*tithe* means "tenth" in Middle English) to the king. This showed that they were loyal to the king. When we give a tenth of our pay to God's purposes, we show our loyalty to God and his kingdom.

Giving means letting go, and letting go of money can be hard. One wise man of God once made this suggestion: "Give until it hurts—and then give until it stops hurting."

And giving does stop hurting. In fact, giving brings great freedom as we control our money rather than having it control us. Giving also brings great joy. Try it and see! With a tithe, show loyalty to your King and know his pleasure and his blessing.

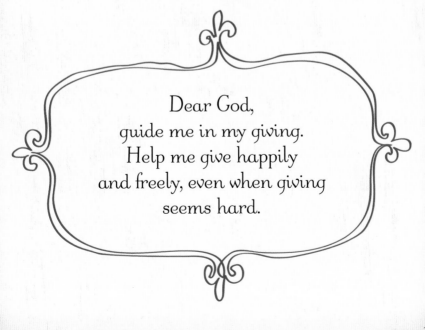

Dear God,
guide me in my giving.
Help me give happily
and freely, even when giving
seems hard.

GIVING MY RESOURCES

Anyone who loves money never has enough.
Anyone who loves wealth is never satisfied with what
they get. That doesn't have any meaning either.

—*Ecclesiastes 5:10*

~~~

"Money never made a man happy yet, nor will it," said Benjamin Franklin, adding, "The more a man has, the more he wants."

Solomon, the wise king of Israel, made that same point long ago: "Whoever loves money never has enough." And that's one reason why giving away our money and possessions is good not only for the receivers but also for us. When we make giving to God's purposes part of our regular spending habits, we honor God. We help people, we keep ourselves from being greedy, and we fight the way our society makes money an idol.

Solomon wrote other words of wisdom regarding the dangers of wealth: Money itself is not evil, but the love of money can lead to sin … More money does not mean more happiness in life … To avoid using money poorly, we are to use what we have for the Lord.

Give generously to the Lord out of the money he has blessed you with. There's no safer way to avoid money's control.

Dear Lord,
I promise to give my
resources to help your plans.

GIVING MY RESOURCES

A poor widow came and put in two very small copper coins. They were worth only a few pennies.

—Mark 12:42

It's an odd thought that being poor is somehow more spiritual than being comfortable or rich. Then there's the idea that a person's great wealth is a sign of God's pleasure. Yet Jesus taught "Is it hard for a camel to go through the eye of a needle? It is even harder for someone who is rich to enter God's kingdom!" (Mark 10:25). After all, it is much harder for a person to recognize the need for God when all his needs and most of his wants are satisfied.

Spiritual health isn't based on money. If anything actually is a sign of spiritual health, it's giving away what God has blessed us with for the good of others in need. Doing so helps us hold our earthly wealth loosely even as it gives God glory.

So what type of giving touches God's heart? Gifts like that of the "poor widow [who] out of her poverty, put in everything—all she had to live on" (vv. 43–44).

If your giving is painless, you may not be giving enough.

Dear God,
I want to give to you. Maybe
I can give money, maybe I
can give time, or maybe I just
give my friendship to someone
who needs it. Help me see how
I can give to serve you.

SHARING MY FAITH

In the same way, let your light shine so others can see it.
Then they will see the good things you do. And they will
bring glory to your Father who is in heaven.

—*Matthew 5:16*

Many of the world's values are upside down. The world goes after money whatever the cost to others. Jesus encourages love whatever the cost to ourselves. The world values making ourselves happy. Jesus values making others happy. The world wants to be served. Jesus values serving.

When we faithfully follow Jesus and obey his commands to love and serve, we are a light in the dark world. Being light means we need to have a humble servant attitude (think "foot washing").

What will you do today to share your faith with acts of love and service?

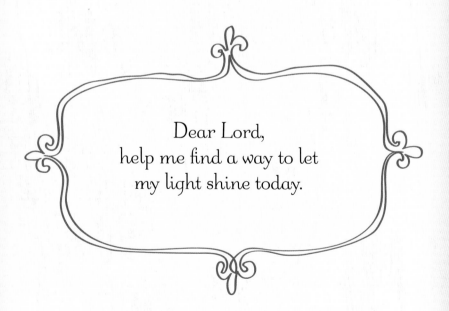

Dear Lord,
help me find a way to let
my light shine today.

SHARING MY FAITH

I haven't kept to myself that what you did for me was right. I have spoken about how faithful you were when you saved me. I haven't hidden your love and your faithfulness from the whole community.

—Psalm 40:10

∽

Sharing our faith is simply telling others who God is and what God has done in our life. You don't have to have a big or "important" story. You don't have to have gone through all sorts of terrible things or had a miracle happen to you. You just need to believe.

Think about young David living out his faith in Almighty God when, with only a sling and some stones, he met and beat the giant Goliath (1 Samuel 17). David shared his faith by the way he lived his life. He also used his words in praise of God's character and acts. In Psalm 40 (above), David celebrated the wonders, deeds, righteousness, faithfulness, and love of God he had experienced.

Like David, in addition to sharing our faith by how we live, we also need to share with words who God is and what great things he has done for us. What's your story?

Dear God
thank you for coming into my life.
Guide me as I tell my story about
how I found you and the wonderful
changes you have made in my life.

IDENTITY IN CHRIST

You will receive power when the Holy Spirit comes on you.
Then you will tell people about me in Jerusalem, and in all
Judea and Samaria. And you will even tell other people
about me from one end of the earth to the other.

—Acts 1:8

"I can't speak in front of people very well." "What if I can't answer her questions?" "I'm new at this Christianity thing." "Witnessing isn't one of my spiritual gifts." These excuses and many others may all be covering up being scared.

But we truly don't need to be afraid. Jesus promises that his Spirit will help us be witnesses for him. So trust the Spirit, speak out in faith that the Spirit is at work, and leave the results in the Spirit's hands.

Remember Jesus' command: "Go and make disciples of all nations" (Matthew 28:19). That didn't include "if that's your comfort zone and area of giftedness." Jesus' command is to everyone who calls him Savior and Lord. All of us are to share the truth about God's love and faithfulness, shown in the life, death, and resurrection of Jesus Christ. Although we may not have a way with words like David or know as much about the law as Paul, God has told us to share our faith. God will give us the power and ability to do so.

Dear Jesus,
thank you for the people who
have shared their faith with me.
Give me the strength to share
my faith with someone new.

153

SHARING MY FAITH

*The Samaritan woman said to [Jesus], "You are a Jew.
I am a Samaritan woman. How can you ask me
for a drink?" She said this because Jews don't
have anything to do with Samaritans.*

—John 4:9

John 4:9 ends with this stark statement: "Jews don't have anything to do with Samaritans." These two peoples really didn't get along. In fact, to avoid the people of Samaria who were living in the region, Jews often went out of their way to cross over the Jordan River and travel on the east side.

No wonder the woman at the well asked the question she did! Jesus—a Jew—was talking to her, a Samaritan! And Jesus said, "Will you give me a drink?" Jesus spoke with her and learned about her life. He also told her about the life she could have with the Lord. As a result, many Samaritans became followers of Christ. They heard Jesus teach and declared, "We know that this man really is the Savior of the world" (v. 42).

Know that there is no one on the planet Jesus doesn't want you sharing the gospel with.

Dear Jesus,
I know you want me to share your Good News with everyone. Help me find a person who needs to hear your Word now.

BE
LIKE
JESUS

LOVE

*The three most important things to have are
faith, hope and love. But the greatest of them is love.*

—1 Corinthians 13:13

What's the main idea of the Bible? What's the bottom-line message of these hundreds of pages? What theme runs throughout the sixty-six books of the Bible that make up God's Word?

You've probably had to find the main idea of stories in school. And if you read a really good book, the author usually has a special message they want you to know or learn. The big yet simple idea behind all the stories and teachings in the Bible—and the answer to the questions above is—love.

Love leads God's story. First Corinthians 13 offers us a description of the love that we see on every page of Scripture. There, the apostle Paul used words like *patient* and *kind* to describe love. He stated that love isn't jealous, boastful, proud, self-seeking, or easily angered. He explained that love "always protects. It always trusts. It always hopes. It never gives up" (v. 7). And if we don't have love, any work we do for the Lord and any way that we serve him or his people is worth nothing.

Dear God,
thank you for filling the Bible
with signs of your love. Thank you
for showing that love in my
life each day.

LOVE

*Love the Lord your God with all your heart
and with all your soul. Love him with all your strength.*

—*Deuteronomy 6:5*

❧

Just before they got to the Promised Land, Moses gathered the Israelites to remind them of what truly mattered in life. He called them to love the Lord with all their being.

Following the command to love God with our whole heart, soul, and strength is the command to "love your neighbor as you love yourself" (Leviticus 19:18).

In Mark 12:29–31, Jesus told the people what the most important commandments were. "Here is the most important one. Moses said, 'Israel, listen to me. The Lord is our God. The Lord is one. Love the Lord your God with all your heart and with all your soul. Love him with all your mind and with all your strength' (Deuteronomy 6:4, 5). And here is the second one. 'Love your neighbor as you love yourself' (Leviticus 19:18). There is no commandment more important than these."

Another time, Jesus took us one step further and said: "Love your enemies. Pray for those who hurt you" (Matthew 5:44).

God loves us, calls us to love him and others, and enables us to do exactly that!

Dear God,
show me how to love my neighbor
as myself, and even to love my
enemies and the people
who have wronged me.

LOVE

But the fruit the Holy Spirit produces is love, joy and peace. It is being patient, kind and good. It is being faithful and gentle and having control of oneself.

—*Galatians 5:22–23*

Like all of his commands to us, God issued his call to love him and to love others for our own good. We are most able to obey God's commands when we ask the Holy Spirit to help us to do what God wants us to do and not do what he doesn't want us to do.

After all, left to our own sinful nature, we would never choose to give others unconditional love. Our first thought is to satisfy our own wants: our personal desires can be more important than the needs and interests of others.

Living a life of love requires the presence of God's love and power within us. When we give in to his presence in our lives, he produces within us love for others that we can't find on our own.

The Bible—including the Old Testament laws, the teachings of Jesus, the wisdom Psalms and Proverbs, and the letters of Paul—provides much instruction regarding how we are to live a life of love. It is God's Spirit that helps us to actually do it.

Dear God
help me to live a life of love.
Help me grow my love for you
and for the people I care about.

LOVE

*Dear friends, let us love one another, because
love comes from God. Everyone who loves has
become a child of God and knows God.*

—1 John 4:7

Love is not something we always do without thinking
about it. We don't love God or other people as naturally
as we breathe or blink. Neither the desire nor the ability
to choose to love is programmed into us. Yet God calls us
again and again in his Word to love him and others.

God—who is himself pure love—does not issue these commands to frustrate or depress us. We need to know, though, that our ability to love begins with receiving God's love for us. We can't give what we don't have. When we are filled with God's love, we are able to love each other. The presence of God's love in us—the presence of his Spirit working in us too—shows that we are in fact God's children.

So, celebrate with John when he wrote: "See what amazing love the Father has given us! Because of it, we are called children of God. And that's what we really are! The world doesn't know us because it didn't know him" (1 John 3:1).

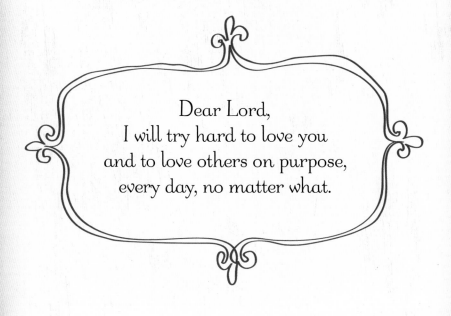

Dear Lord,
I will try hard to love you
and to love others on purpose,
every day, no matter what.

JOY

*You always show me the path of life. You will
fill me with joy when I am with you. You will make
me happy forever at your right hand.*

—Psalm 16:11

Sometimes life seems hard, unfair, and meaningless. Jesus
warned his followers they would experience hard times,
and today we run into some of the same tough situations
and not-so-nice people. The world isn't perfect, and from
time to time we all feel pain.

In the Bible we find singing, dancing, and shouts of joy at
times of celebration, but what about the ordinary times?
Can we still find joy in the boring moments of life? What
about in the hard times too?

God showers us with blessings that bring joy to our lives,
but true joy is not found in those gifts. True joy is found
only in God himself. When we feed on his Word, live
according to his commands, and trust in his promises, we
find joy.

So may we wisely open up God's Word to find the path
of life God has for us and be guided by his presence.
Whatever is happening, we can turn to God's Word and
find joy.

Dear God,
help me find joy in the good
times and bad. Help me find joy in
you and in your Word.

JOY

I have told you this so that you will have the same joy that I have. I also want your joy to be complete.

—John 15:11

What, according to Jesus, is key to our knowing his joy?

Let's back up and see: "Just as the Father has loved me, I have loved you. Now remain in my love. If you obey my commands, you will remain in my love. In the same way, I have obeyed my Father's commands and remain in his love. I have told you this …" (vv. 9–11).

We feel joy when we receive God's love and remain in his love by keeping his commands. Sounds simple enough, but this is not an easy assignment for human beings. We like being in charge of our lives. And that struggle doesn't end when we name Jesus our Savior and ask him to be our Lord.

But when we do obey Christ's commands, his nutrients of joy run through our spiritual veins from the inside out and produce the sweet fruit of joy in our lives.

Not convinced? Then make an effort today—and each day—to live in Christ by obeying his commands. If you walk through a day mindful of his presence and love, you can know joy.

Dear Lord,
I will live a life of joy
by obeying your commands.

PEACE

Look at the birds of the air. They don't plant or gather crops. They don't put away crops in storerooms. But your Father who is in heaven feeds them. Aren't you worth much more than they are?

—Matthew 6:26

When you hear the word worry, what do you think of? A certain thing that happened? A person in your life? Do you get a funny feeling in your stomach? Does your heart beat quickly?

Worry takes the peace from our lives. But Jesus, our Prince of Peace, shows us how God can love and care for us. He doesn't want worries of this life to overwhelm us, his children.

Do the birds, Jesus asked, worry about where their next meal will come from? Do the "flowers of the field" worry about how pretty they are? No! So why should we worry?

When you see a bird or flower during the day, remember that God cares for us in the same way he cares for them.

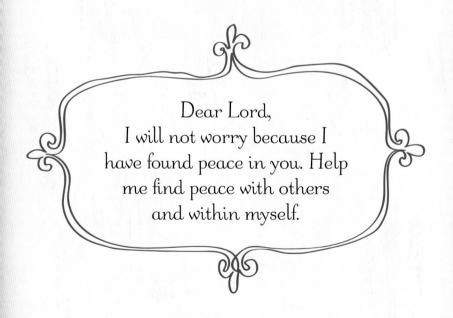

Dear Lord,
I will not worry because I have found peace in you. Help me find peace with others and within myself.

PEACE

Abram said to Lot, "Let's not argue with each other. The people taking care of your herds and those taking care of mine shouldn't argue with one another either. After all, we're part of the same family."

—*Genesis 13:8*

Abram and Lot had moved their families from Egypt, through the desert, and into Bethel. Lot was Abram's nephew, and both were very rich.

"But the land didn't have enough food for both Abram and Lot. They had large herds and many servants, so they weren't able to stay together. The people who took care of Abram's herds and those who took care of Lot's herds began to argue" (Genesis 13:6–7).

Abram chose to calm their fight. Even though Abram was older and should have had first pick of the land, he put peace in the family above his own wishes. He let Lot choose first.

Now think about your own life. Are there times when you could set aside your own needs or what you think is "fair" in order to keep the peace with your family or friends?

Dear God,
I promise to do what is
kind and right by putting the
needs of others before
my own needs.

PEACE

*Let us stop judging one another. Instead, decide
not to put anything in the way of a brother
or sister. Don't put anything in their
way that would make them trip and fall.*

—Romans 14:13,19

It is pretty easy to get annoyed by other people. It's
certainly easier than looking at what we might be doing
to annoy them. And we also might not be able to see that
we're doing or saying something that makes it hard for
other believers to follow their walk with God.

God wants us to "make every effort to do what leads to
peace." The first step may be to ask him to show us what
we do that gets in the way of peace. Then we can work on
changing those unhelpful behaviors. One good result will
be enjoying peace with our brothers and sisters in Christ.

Dear Lord,
please show me the things
I do that hurt, worry, or challenge
the people around me. Then
help me change my ways.

SELF-CONTROL

Delilah said to Samson, "Tell me the secret of why you are so strong." She continued to pester him day after day. She nagged him until he was sick and tired of it. So he told her everything.

—Judges 16:6,16–17

Samson loved Delilah, even though she didn't believe in his God. He had no self-control and couldn't keep his secret. He forgot his promise to God. His lack of self-control led to his capture. Samson let his feelings for Delilah get in the way of his promise to God.

Think about the ways that you might lack self-control. Do you eat more cookies than you should? Do you take more than one free candy at the bank? Do you have a hard time putting down the tablet when gaming time is over?

It's hard for us to keep ourselves under control. But if we let God control our actions, we can stay away from sin or poor choices.

Dear God,
help me practice self-control.
I never want a small problem—
or a big one—to keep me
from doing what is right.

HOPE

*In Jerusalem there was a man named Simeon. He was a
good and godly man. He was waiting for God's promise
to Israel to come true ... The Spirit had told Simeon
that he would not die before he had seen the Lord's Messiah.*

—Luke 2:25–26

Mary and Joseph brought their new baby to Jerusalem to
present him to the Lord at the temple. This was Hebrew
tradition. They brought an offering of two doves.

Simeon had waited his whole life for God to fulfill his
promise. He had hope that had never diminished. God's
promise to send his Son was his greatest promise. And God
is a promise-keeper. When Simeon saw Jesus, he knew
immediately that God had kept his promise. He knew his
life was complete and he could pass on in peace.

Just as Simeon trusted God, you can trust in God and his
promises. Jesus came to bring us hope. He is a reminder
that God will never, ever leave us. So let God's whispers
into your heart and have hope.

Dear Jesus,
because of you I can face
every good and bad thing
in life with hope.

PATIENCE

*Lead a life worthy of the Lord ... very strong,
in keeping with his glorious power. We want you to
be patient. We pray that you will never give up.*

Colossians 1:10–11

Waiting is hard, isn't it? It can feel like forever to have to
wait for dinner when you are hungry. Or to have to wait to
get a cool new toy until it's your birthday. Why is waiting
so hard? Because we can quickly run out of patience with
others and even God when things aren't going our way.

Have you ever tried to rush things, rush God, or rush other
people? How did that work out? If we are impatient, we
might miss God, each other, and life. Have you noticed that
God never seems to be in much of a hurry? Why should we
be?

Life is a long trip with God and each other. Life is not
perfect and neither are we. We will need patience to get
through it. Our God promises to help us.

So let's take God up on his promise. He promises we will
all get there on time and enjoy each other along the way.

Dear God,
help me to be patient, especially
when it's hard. Help me see beyond
the needs of today and into
the needs of tomorrow.

KINDNESS/GOODNESS

"Don't be afraid," David told him. "You can be sure that I will be kind to you because of your father Jonathan. I'll give back to you all the land that belonged to your grandfather Saul. And I'll always provide what you need."

—2 Samuel 9:7

David's best friend Jonathan had died long ago. But David and Jonathan's friendship was so great that David still missed his friend. He wanted to do something to honor Jonathan's memory. David found out that one of Jonathan's sons was still alive but that he was injured and needed kindness. David told Mephibosheth that he wanted him to live in the palace. And he gave him all the land that had once belonged to his grandfather, Saul.

David was a man after God's own heart. And God's heart is kind and good. God wants our hearts to be like his. Think carefully about how you treat others. Are all your actions done out of kindness? What have you done lately that might not have been so kind? Can you make it better?

Think about making a promise today to God to always act with a kind heart.

Dear Lord,
I choose to be kind and good
in my relationships with others.

183

FAITHFULNESS

"I serve the Lord," Mary answered.
"May it happen to me just as you said it would."

—Luke 1:38

Can you imagine being asked to do something so important that the whole future of the world depended on it? That's what it was like for Mary. The angel Gabriel appeared to her and told her she would give birth to the Messiah. That must have been a scary idea to her. She wasn't married. And she was being trusted with a huge responsibility. But Mary had faith that the Lord had good plans for her and for her son. And she was faithful to God and accepted his blessing.

God may not be giving you such a big responsibility. But he does ask you to stay faithful to him no matter what life brings your way. Can you be loyal to God and to your brothers and sisters in Christ? Can you keep your promises to God and to others?

Dear Lord,
I trust in you. Help others trust
in me. Help me keep my promises
to you and to the people I care about.

GENTLENESS

*David sent some messengers from the desert to
give his greetings to our master. But Nabal shouted
at them and was rude to them.*

1 Samuel 25:14

❧

Are you known for your gentleness and thoughtfulness
with others? Or are you one of those people that others
avoid in tough times?

Nabal was a mean guy. David and his men had protected
Nabal's flocks and lands, but when David came asking
for a favor, Nabal was rude. Nabal was only saved from
David's anger by the gentle actions of his wife, Abigail.
Abigail heard about Nabal's rudeness and rushed out to
offer an apology and gifts to David.

God loves it when we treat others with gentleness. When
we consider the needs and feelings of others, we please
God. And being calm and gentle with others makes us feel
good on the inside too.

Dear God,
I promise to be thoughtful,
considerate, and calm with others.

HUMILITY

*He appeared as a man. He was humble and
obeyed God completely. He did this even though
it led to his death. Even worse, he died on a cross!*

—Philippians 2:8

The apostle Paul wrote a letter to the church in Philippi.
He asked the believers there to be humble. To be humble
means to not think you are a lot better than others. Jesus is
a good example of a humble man.

Today, people often think that being humble means you
are weak or that you let people walk all over you. Or they
think it means you don't think very much of yourself.

Humility is choosing to think that others are more important than yourself. When we have accepted God's love
and care, it is easier to care for others. We should have no
doubt that God values us. When we know that, we can
help others with their needs.

Dear Jesus,
help me to follow in your
footsteps. Help me choose to be
humble and to value others
more than myself.

HUMILITY

So he got up from the meal and took off his outer clothes. He wrapped a towel around his waist. After that, he poured water into a large bowl. Then he began to wash his disciples' feet. He dried them with the towel that was wrapped around him.

—John 13:4–5

The "he" in this story is Jesus. In Jesus' day people walked on dusty roads wherever they needed to go. Their feet were filthy by the end of the day. Washing those filthy feet was a job given to slaves. And that happened before the beginning of meal time.

Everything was ready for Jesus' last supper with his disciples. Well, almost everything … No one was there to wash the feet of those gathering to share the meal. None of the twelve disciples took on the task. After all, they were well aware that they were among the Master's inner circle. They were the special ones. Foot washing was always the task of the lowest servant in a household.

Imagine the disciples' surprise when Jesus stood up from the table and prepared to wash their feet. Imagine your Bible study leader or your pastor washing your feet.

Their beloved Jesus took on the task. When he finished, he said, "You should do as I have done for you."

May we serve as Jesus served. We should never think of any task as too dirty or low. Every job honors God.

Dear God,
I promise to look for opportunities
to serve the people in my life. I
want to do good for others,
even if that means taking on
a task no one else will.